CODE

Amazing Architecture

Charlotte Guillain

Contents

Made you look! .... page 5
Strange shapes .... page 6
Animal inspiration .... page 10
Plant power .... page 14
Time for tea .... page 16
Bold and bright .... page 18
Invisible inspiration .... page 20
Accidental look-a-like .... page 22
Glossary/Index .... page 23

OXFORD
UNIVERSITY PRESS

Mini, Macro and Micro World!

Hello. My name is **Mini Marvel**. My dad **Macro Marvel** and I invented **Micro World**. This is the book that inspired us to make **Marvel Towers**.

My dad Macro Marvel

You are here

Did you know?

Sometimes a smaller photo is used with a main photo so you can compare the two.

Plant power

This structure was designed to **resemble** a flower called a lotus. It's made up of 27 petal shapes.

The whole structure looks like it is floating on the water, like a real lotus flower.

a lotus flower

14

Fact!

The Burj Khalifa in Dubai is currently the world's tallest building. It is 828 metres tall!

Mini's Top Spot

Can you find this word in the index?

glass

Can you look up the page that it appears on?

3

Before you read

Word alert

- Look at the words. Here are the sounds to remember when you are reading this book:

whole   w**ar**m   w**a**ter
h**al**t   w**a**tch

- Look out for more words with these sounds when you are reading.

What does it mean?

architect – person who designs structures as a job
structure – anything that has been built

Into the zone

- Have you ever seen a building in the shape of a fish? How about a teapot?

4

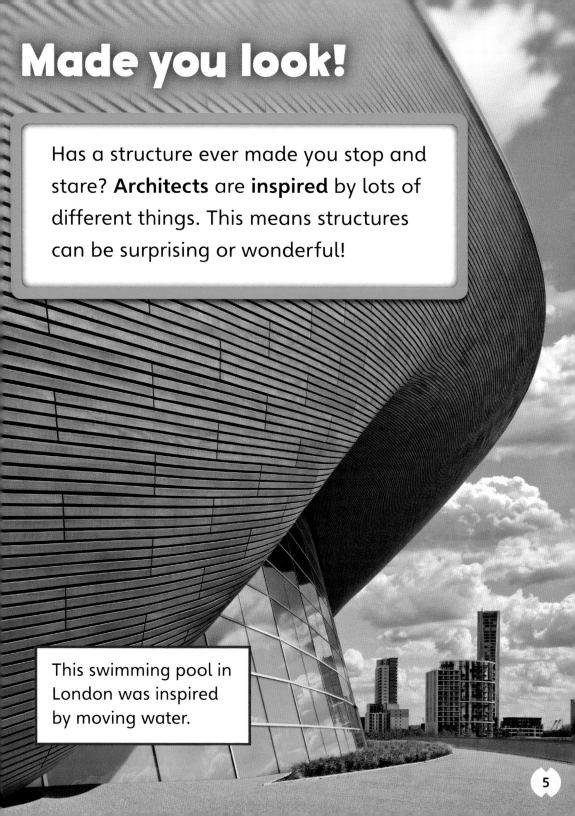

Made you look!

Has a structure ever made you stop and stare? **Architects** are **inspired** by lots of different things. This means structures can be surprising or wonderful!

This swimming pool in London was inspired by moving water.

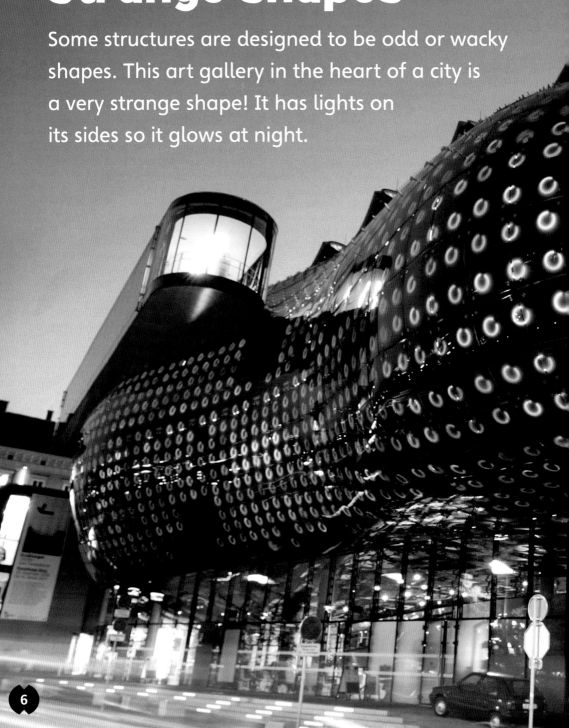

Strange shapes

Some structures are designed to be odd or wacky
shapes. This art gallery in the heart of a city is
a very strange shape! It has lights on
its sides so it glows at night.

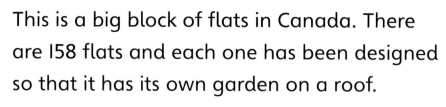

This is a big block of flats in Canada. There are 158 flats and each one has been designed so that it has its own garden on a roof.

This structure is nicknamed the Bird's Nest because of its shape. It is in China and was made for the 2008 Olympic Games. It is strong enough to survive an earthquake! Now, pop concerts are held here as well as sporting events.

This structure has been constructed from metal and plastic. It is designed to last for a hundred years.

80,000 people can sit inside and watch football or athletics.

Animal inspiration

This crocodile-shaped hotel looks like it is about to start crawling across the park! Would you like to stay in the belly of a crocodile?

Crocodiles live in warm places, so this hotel is in a very hot part of the world.

Can you guess what the people who work here do?
They help fishermen and others who work on water.
Their jobs are all about fish!

I look like I swallowed all the workers!

This structure opened in 2012.

This is a **tourist** information centre in New Zealand. It is constructed from sheets of metal. The structure was inspired by the dogs used to herd and move sheep on the farms in New Zealand.

There's a huge sheep next to the dog, too.

Plant power

This structure was designed to **resemble** a flower called a lotus. It's made up of 27 petal shapes.

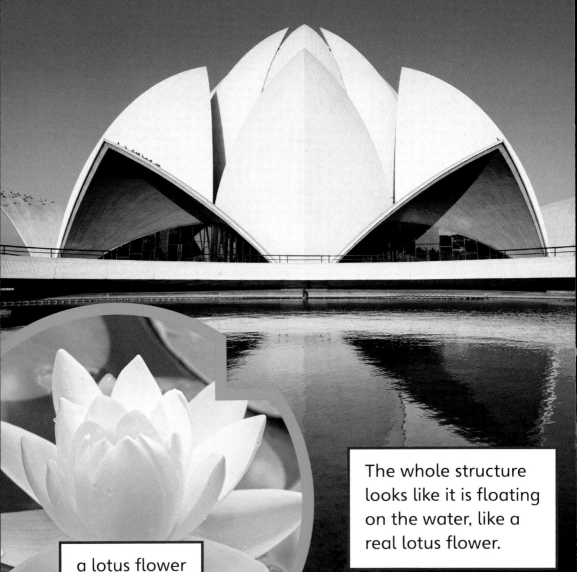

a lotus flower

The whole structure looks like it is floating on the water, like a real lotus flower.

This structure is in Scotland. It was constructed a very long time ago, in 1761 – so it is over 250 years old! Back then, pineapples were rare in Scotland.

13.7 metres

The pineapple is made from stone.

Time for tea

How can you make a teapot interesting? By making it extremely tall! This gigantic teapot-shaped structure is in China, where tea is a popular drink.

39 metres

The teapot is made out of metal sheets and stained glass. It has 10 floors!

Bold and bright

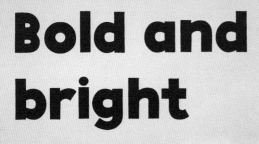

You might think of **power plants** as ugly, smoky places that make people cough, but this one is different. It has been covered in bright patterns and strange shapes. It burns rubbish to heat over 60,000 homes.

These structures are in a park in Spain. The park opened to the public in 1926, but many people still visit it today. There are lots of sculptures and bright tiles to look at.

Invisible inspiration

Some structures are hard to see. They are designed to blend in! This hotel room in Sweden is high up in a forest. It is covered with mirrors that reflect its surroundings so that the room is not easy to spot.

The hotel room is not the only structure to use mirrors to hide itself. This visitor centre is at a **botanical gardens**. Mirrors face towards the trees so the centre is nearly invisible.

Accidental look-a-like

Sometimes, structures look like an **alternative** object to the one the architect intended! This Chinese skyscraper is supposed to resemble a gateway. Many people think the two towers look like a pair of shiny trousers!

300 metres

If you were an architect, what would inspire you?

Glossary

alternative	different, or another possibility
architect	person who designs structures as a job
botanical gardens	where plants are grown for science and for people to look at
inspire	make someone want to do something
power plant	structure that makes electric power
resemble	to look like someone or something

Index

flats	7
glass	17
hotel	10, 20
lights	6
metal	8, 12, 17
mirrors	20–21
plastic	8

Now you have read ...
Amazing Architecture

Reflect on your reading

Think about all the structures you have read about.
Which one would you most like to visit?
Which one is the most unusual?

Use the information

Look back through the book to help you fill in the missing pieces
of information on this table.
Try describing each structure in your own words.

What inspired it?	What is it used for?	How would you describe it?
moving water (page 5)	swimming pool	curving, glass looks like water
(page 10)		
(page 12)		
(page 17)		

Think about the information

Read page 15 again.
Why do you think they made this building in the shape of
a pineapple?

24